François Martial Elysée Tsanga

Bank liquidity and financing of the economy in the CEMAC zone

François Martial Elysée Tsanga

Bank liquidity and financing of the economy in the CEMAC zone

ScienciaScripts

Imprint

Any brand names and product names mentioned in this book are subject to trademark, brand or patent protection and are trademarks or registered trademarks of their respective holders. The use of brand names, product names, common names, trade names, product descriptions etc. even without a particular marking in this work is in no way to be construed to mean that such names may be regarded as unrestricted in respect of trademark and brand protection legislation and could thus be used by anyone.

Cover image: www.ingimage.com

This book is a translation from the original published under ISBN 978-620-2-27567-5.

Publisher:
Sciencia Scripts
is a trademark of
Dodo Books Indian Ocean Ltd. and OmniScriptum S.R.L publishing group

120 High Road, East Finchley, London, N2 9ED, United Kingdom
Str. Armeneasca 28/1, office 1, Chisinau MD-2012, Republic of Moldova, Europe
Printed at: see last page
ISBN: 978-620-5-84374-1

Table of Contents

General Introduction

Background and rationale

The most recurrent concern of central banks is the possibility that abundant bank liquidity could impede the ability of monetary policy to affect the level of economic activity or inflation (Agénor and El Aynaoui, 2009). In most financial systems, excess liquidity can be defined as an involuntary accumulation of reserves by commercial banks. Thus, although banks may prefer to hold reserves above or beyond what is required by banking law (to meet potential unexpected cash withdrawals by their customers, for example), excess liquidity only occurs if they reluctantly hold more liquidity than they desire.

In a crisis environment, characterized by changing volatility, demand for reserves may rise sharply-either for precautionary reasons or because banks find it too risky to lend (risk aversion)[2] . This observation, as argued by Agénor et al. (2004), demonstrates a useful starting point for identifying the source of credit contraction: if banks are unwilling, rather than unable, to extend loans, a credit contraction may come from the supply side of factors, rather than the demand side.

From an analytical perspective, it is convenient to classify the main drivers of excess liquidity into structural or cyclical determinants. The first structural factor that is commonly identified is low financial development or financial deepening (M2/GDP). In countries with poorly developed financial sectors, banks (and their customers) tend to have a high demand for liquidity. In particular, instability in payment systems may lead banks to prefer to hold relatively large reserves to help regulate their liquidity needs.

The costs of information retrieval, project appraisal, and borrower supervision can also be relatively high; and this can complicate liquidity management and thus can lead to reserve accumulation beyond desired levels. This is one of the most widely accepted explanations for the persistently high level of bank reserves in low-income

---

2 Ashcraft et al (2009), for example, found that during the 2007-2008 financial crisis in the United States, banks increased their reserve holdings (the process of restricting lending) as a precautionary measure against liquidity shocks.

countries in Central Africa, where portfolio allocation opportunities are limited (Saxegaard, 2006). A second factor is the high degree of risk aversion, which leads to high risk premiums and low credit demand. The degree of risk aversion can be directly related to chronic macroeconomic instability, and this would explain the positive correlation between high inflation and excess liquidity.

Inflation can also represent a cyclical cause of excess liquidity. The importance of the latter is accompanied by a high volatility of relative prices (and therefore an increase in the risks of investment projects characterized by a high degree of irreversibility), an excess in inflation can increase uncertainty about the value of the collateral of borrowers - large banks, when faced with problems of adverse selection, either set a high risk premium or increases the incidence of credit rationing. This is because, in the formal case, a high lending rate will lead to a contraction in the demand for credit, and both reactions can result in an unintended accumulation of excess reserves.

Another important cyclical factor is a significant inflow of capital initiated by the banking system. Over the past two decades, a number of developing countries, both low- and middle-income, have introduced measures to encourage asymmetric capital account openness (i.e., the lifting of restrictions on capital movements for non-residents, while extensive controls on foreign currency transactions by residents are maintained). In many cases these measures lead to a large flow of capital, often associated with the privatization of state-owned enterprises. In Guyana, for example, financial liberalization was accompanied in the late 1990s by a considerable increase in excess liquidity (Khemraj, 2007). In Morocco, a large number of privatizations and the increase in foreign direct investment (FDI) have led in recent years to a significant increase in liquidity in the banking system, causing the Central Bank to increase reserve requirements abruptly in order to avoid the development of inflationary pressure (Agénor and El Aynaoui, 2007).

With regard to financing the economy, an accelerated economic growth strategy requires, in addition to the implementation of appropriate reforms and policies, an increase in productive investments. This observation, unanimously shared by the

CEMAC Heads of State, raises the fundamental question of the availability of financing. It is clear from certain experiences (Latin America, Asia and in developed countries) that banks play a fundamental role in financing the economy, specifically in financing the private sector, the engine of economic growth. This indispensable role expected of banks, in particular, and of financial markets in general, shows the interest for the Member States of the Union to ensure both the stability of the banking sector and to see to it that this sector contributes more to the coverage of the financing needs of the economy and particularly those of companies.

To this end, the BEAC has taken concrete steps to create conditions conducive to a significant participation of the CEMAC financial sector in financing the economic activities of member states. The subregion's banking system must respond to the economic problems of member states by addressing concerns about the under-financing of the zone's economies.

The CEMAC banking system is experiencing excess liquidity in contrast to the underdeveloped situation in which all its member countries find themselves. These countries, most of which are among the poorest in the world, have a productive sector and SMEs that frequently lack the financing necessary for their development. This gives them mediocre economic performance in terms of growth compared to other Third World countries. The quantitative theory of money, and even more so the new classical economics, with the problem of the temporal incoherence of monetary policy, have validated the inflationary paradigm of monetary creation ex nihilo.

Given the weakness of the tax base of the countries in the zone, there is only one possibility left for them to consider financing development projects: mobilizing domestic and foreign savings. To encourage this approach, measures have been developed to restore budgetary balance, with the notion of "intertemporal solvency" in fiscal policy, and monetary balance, with an increase in interest rates to encourage savings. The financing of the economy can only come from prior savings.

Such an analysis associating underdevelopment with low savings neglects the difficulties of access to credit for businesses linked to the specific nature of the banking market in the CEMAC countries. In these countries, it is not the resources that are lacking, but the intermediation mechanism that consists in transforming resources into loans to agents in need of financing. Banks behave in a way that slows down the economic circuit. With high profitability in an oligopolistic market, they prefer to keep idle capacity rather than lend part of the savings collected from customers. The result is a situation of excess liquidity, which is reflected in the increase in their deposits with the Central Bank.

The establishment of two regional stock exchanges and the recourse of governments to internal debt have not made it possible to fully absorb the excess liquidity of banks. This excess liquidity is combined with the difficulty of access to credit for SMEs and the productive sector. In Cameroon, for example, it is estimated that out of 93,969 active businesses, nearly 95% face financing constraints (RGE, 2009).

Given the importance of SMEs in sub-Saharan African countries, which account for 50% of GDP and employment, financing constraints have been considered by some studies to be the main obstacle to the development of these countries, ahead of the problems of corruption and inadequate infrastructure [(aryeetey, 1998), (Africapractice, 2005)]. This statement is probably not excessive, especially since difficulties in accessing credit are not limited to SMEs. A large part of the private sector is affected by this problem. Credits granted to this sector represent only 15% of GDP, compared to 27% in South Asia and 109% in high-income countries (LEFILLEUR, 2007, p.68).

Issue

The importance and the stakes involved in the issue of access to credit led the Bank of Central African States (BEAC) to hold "consultations on bank financing of the economy in the CEMAC countries". The conclusions of these consultations were not followed by measures that would have brought about a real change in the behavior of banks. The issue of under-financing of businesses therefore remains a central issue in Africa, particularly in the CEMAC countries where it rhymes with the excess liquidity of the banking system. This is why it is necessary to highlight the importance of bank liquidity in financing the economy.

Research Questions

It is therefore imperative to ask the following question:

Main question

What are the factors in the banking sector that significantly influence the financing of the economy in the CEMAC zone?

Specific questions

• Does the excess liquidity of banks in the sub-region influence the financing of the economy?

• What is the relationship between reserve requirements and the financing of the economy?

• How does the lending rate affect the financing of the economy in the CEMAC zone?

• How does inflation affect the financing of the economy?

• Does the increase in financial deepening affect the financing of the economy?

• Does the increase in net foreign assets influence the financing of the economy?

Objectives of the study

The objectives of this study will be:

Main objective

The main objective of this study is to determine the factors in the banking sector that significantly influence the financing of the economy in the CEMAC zone.

Specific objectives

Specifically, it will measure the impact of variables such as reserve requirements, lending rates, inflation, financial deepening and banks' net foreign assets on the financing of the economy in the CEMAC zone.

Research Hypotheses

In order to achieve these objectives, the following assumptions were made:

Main hypothesis

H_0: The excess liquidity of banks in the CEMAC zone reduces the financing of the economies of its member countries.

Secondary hypotheses

H_1: Excess reserve requirements and increased financial deepening improve the financing of the economy in the CEMAC zone.

H_2: The increase in the lending rate, inflation, and net foreign assets reduces the financing of the economy in the CEMAC zone.

Interest of the study

At a time when most countries in the CEMAC zone have developed strategies for economic emergence and are resorting to private savings to finance their so-called structural projects, it is important to look at the availability of the banking system in terms of savings mobilization. It is also important to look at the relationship between this level of bank liquidity and the financing of the economy. In such a context, this study is of interest insofar as it analyzes this relationship and serves as a guide to public authorities in the development of their economic policy.

In fact, by establishing a relationship between the factors of the banking sector and the financing of the economy, this study highlights the levers on which the public authorities could act to take advantage of the very high liquidity of banks in the subregion in financing the economies of the zone.

Review of the literature

Despite the importance of the issue for the BEAC, and especially for the heads of CEMAC member states, there are few writings or articles that have attempted to explore analytically the implications of excess liquidity on the financing of the economy. However, this issue is not new in the economic literature. Thus, we can cite the work of Fouda Owoundi, in his article "*Bank overliquidity in the franc zone: how to explain the CEMAC paradox*"; Soumaila Doumbia, in his article on "*The underfinancing of firms in a context of bank overliquidity: le paradoxe de l'UEMOA*"; Alberto Giovannini, in his article "*Monetary policy, liquidity, and foreign exchange markets*" and Agénor and El Aynaoui in their article on "Excess *liquidity, bank pricing rules, and monetary policy*".

Methodology

To answer this question, this study opts for a panel data analysis in which the credit to the economy variable measures the financing of the economy, while the explanatory variables measure the liquidity of banks.

We will try to see how they affect the bank financing of the economy.

The structure of the selected model is inspired by Demirgüç-Kunt & Huizinga (1999). It is a linear model, where the credit variable on the economy is the dependent variable. The explanatory variables retained are: reserves, lending rate, financial deepening, inflation, net foreign assets. In addition, our work focuses on the CEMAC countries over a twenty-year period (20 years) from 1986 to 2006. The data used is obtained from the World Bank 2008 database (WDI, 2008).

Scope and limitations of the study

This study takes into account all CEMAC countries and uses 2008 World Bank data. However, the complexity of these data and the problems of missing data observed in the use of the database are in themselves one of the limitations of the study.

Proposed plan

Following this general introduction, this report will contain four chapters. The first will present the economic and financial situation of the CEMAC. The second will focus on the theoretical foundations and the review of the literature on the relationship between the liquidity of the banking system and the financing of the economy. The third chapter will present the methodology that will allow us to analyze and interpret the empirical results. In the fourth chapter we will present the results obtained in order to give an answer to our research question. The work will end with a general conclusion.

CHAPTER I: ECONOMIC AND FINANCIAL SITUATION OF CEMAC

Introduction

CEMAC is composed of six member states: Cameroon, Chad, Central African Republic, Congo, Gabon and Equatorial Guinea. It is characterized not only by the fixed parity of the CFA franc with the euro, but also by its unlimited convertibility and, above all, by the obligation of its central bank to deposit at least 50% of its foreign exchange reserves in the so-called operations account, opened at the Bank of France, in return for the guarantee given by the French Treasury[3] . As a key mechanism in the zone, this account determines monetary policy through the level of reserves and thus provides a framework for monetary creation.

The statutes of the central banks also provide for a limit on the advances they can make to national treasuries, depending on the state of public finances. The current economic situation in the zone is not very bright. Despite the stability of the macroeconomic framework, the reforms undertaken after the crisis have not produced satisfactory results, especially in terms of growth and poverty reduction.

I- The economic performance of the CEMAC zone

The recent history of the zone is marked by serious economic and financial problems, which it faced from the early 1980s onwards, and which resulted in large budget and operating account deficits, severe bank illiquidity, rapid inflation, overvalued exchange rates and heavy external and internal government indebtedness. This crisis has been widely debated and has led to calls for institutional reforms. Among these reforms is integration, which is seen as a useful step toward opening up the zone to the world market and liberalizing trade.

Unfortunately, the results of this convergence of economies have been disappointing to date, as shown by some studies (Fouda Owoundi, 2008). The example of CEMAC

---

3 Initially 65%, this fraction was reduced in 2007 to 50%.

is quite illustrative in this regard. The progress of major community projects, such as the construction of the common market, infrastructure development, etc., is disappointing to say the least. Indeed, while it is true that the Generalized Preferential Tariff (GPT) established in 1994 reached zero in 1998 among the six member states, intra-community trade has not made significant progress. Trade with other African countries accounted for only about 6% of total external trade flows between 1995 and 2005, while intra-community trade accounted for barely 3% of the total value of trade, or CFAF 119 billion[4].

This performance, far from being the result of chance, is due to several factors, the most important of which are certainly linked to policies based on national preferences and to the problem of infrastructure, as noted by the United Nations Economic Commission for Africa (2007) with regard to the landlocked nature of certain states (Chad, Central African Republic) and the very poor connection of national networks of all kinds.

Moreover, while the countries have recorded overall positive real growth rates in recent years (5.5 percent in 2005 compared to 3.3 percent in 2006 for CEMAC as a whole), as well as a significant improvement in the macroeconomic framework, the most recent studies agree that this has gone hand in hand with a low level of human development, resulting, according to Avom and Carmignagni (2008), in an abnormally high level of poverty and a deepening of inequalities. According to the same authors, the average distance between poor incomes and the poverty line is constantly increasing.

It should also be noted that unlike the economy of the WAEMU zone, which appears to be relatively more diversified, with a range of agricultural exports (mainly cotton, cocoa and coffee), food crops (rice, millet, cassava, yams) and a comparatively well-developed secondary sector (agri-food industries, textile industry, construction and public works), the economy of the CEMAC zone as a whole is heavily dependent on oil, whose revenues are increasingly feeding into the resources of the states (49.13%

---

4 BEAC, in: Comité monétaire la Zone franc, Rapport annuel 2006

in 2002 and 70% in 2006).

Table 1: Financial operations of CEMAC States

Titles	2002	2003	2004	2005	2006
Total revenues (in billions of FCFA)	3536	3688.7	4246.4	6069	7933.6
Oil revenues (in %)	49. 13	47.46	53.58	63.58	70.04

Source: National administrations, IMF and BEAC

In this respect, the trade balance is structurally in surplus depending on the price situation, and is highly volatile, with a high sensitivity of public budget balances to price fluctuations, which is all the greater given the fluctuating value of the dollar against the euro. Added to this is the weight of the informal sector in the economies, which has the disadvantage of reducing the tax base and therefore the tax revenues likely to finance the production of public goods necessary for this form of growth. It should also be noted that this sector itself suffers from exclusion from access to credit.

As can be understood, the current challenges for CEMAC lie, on the one hand, in identifying appropriate public policies and, on the other hand, in resolving the broader problem of development financing. Unlike WAEMU, where significant efforts have been made to pursue an active fiscal policy that respects the debt constraint, CEMAC has not yet succeeded in making a structural change in the way its economies are financed. Monetary financing of governments by the BEAC remains in force. However, this method of financing runs counter to recent economic debates on the independence of the Central Bank, and in any event remains very limited as a source of financing to support an active policy to fight poverty. Following the example of the WAEMU countries, which have increasingly resorted to domestic financing through the issuance of public securities on the subregional financial market since 1998, the CEMAC member countries are increasingly resorting to this type of financing, given the excess liquidity of their banks.

While it should be noted that the excess liquidity of banks is a development factor, insofar as they not only use their excess liquidity to purchase public and private securities, but above all contribute through these operations to lowering the financial conditions of funds raised by governments and the private sector. In the CEMAC zone, on the other hand, the problem of excess bank liquidity remains unresolved, despite the economic situation outlined above and the fact that developing countries are currently victims of a crowding out effect on international capital markets. While the existence of significant financial needs on the part of both governments and the private sector makes this excess liquidity paradoxical, it is even more so because practice is far from conforming to the teachings of economic theory.

II- Bank overliquidity in the CEMAC zone

Within the framework of the CEMAC, COBAC Regulation R-93/06 on the liquidity of institutions has established several liquidity ratios, in particular the liquidity ratio and the long-term transformation coefficient. The latter is a standard that aims to oblige banks to respect a minimum ratio between their assets and liabilities with more than five years to maturity and their resources of the same nature.

The minimum set is 50%. But this minimum does not capture either immediate or potential bank liquidity. This is why it is appropriate to refer to the liquidity ratio, which requires banks to respect a minimum ratio between their liquid assets and liabilities of less than one month. At all times, banks must have a liquidity ratio of at least 100%. Thus, any bank whose liquidity ratio is above this threshold can be considered to be overliquid. As shown in Table 3, it appears that all CEMAC banks have been in this situation since 1995.

Table 2: Liquidity ratio of CEMAC banks (average per country in %)

Country	1995	1996	1997	1998	1999	2000	2001	2002	2003	2004	2005	2006	2007
Chad	221,12	239,87	242,47	303,43	250,47	112,4	180,5	174,9	211,8	204,8	178,8	281,3	230,5
Guinea Eq	265,69	283,42	229,92	186,19	212,84	217,8	244,2	253,3	333,3	275,8	322,7	310,5	303,8
Gabon	154,78	200,57	135,95	134,34	135,63	144,1	128	139,6	185,3	219,5	232,1	210,4	198,8
RCA	204,06	207,36	211,08	195,63	175,69	127	72	73,7	86,2	119,9	165,1	149,7	182,8
Cameroon	110,98	107,7	141,56	122,03	136,71	169,4	156,4	206,4	185,9	197,6	203,5	231,8	242,8
Congo						336,7	181,6	156,1	126,8	175,2	287,6	293,5	337,8
CEMAC						174,5	151,1	182,4	191,2	206,8	233,2	244,5	239

Source: *Commission Bancaire de l'Afrique Centrale (average calculation per country made on an exceptional basis and having the advantage of preserving the*

This excess liquidity can also be measured by other indicators, such as the banks' cash balance (st), the liquidity ratio (rl), the level of refinancing with the BEAC (ref), and the balance of transactions with customers (soc). The paradox of excess liquidity is illustrated by the graph - bank excess liquidity and credit to the economy in CEMAC 1993-2006, which traces the evolution of these different indicators (with : ST = st/b measuring excess liquidity; REF = ref/b, refinancing; CRED = cred/b, credits to the economy; and ET = et/b, cash uses). These indicators are considered as a percentage of total assets (b). The graph below provides a good illustration of the evolution of bank liquidity in the sub-region, as well as the evolution of financing of the economy.

The chart, which is based on aggregated data from the balance sheets and income statements of CEMAC banks, shows in particular the evolution of the amount of credit granted by the banks - based on the amounts outstanding on their balance sheets (cred) - compared to the evolution of their cash uses (and). At the same time, their cash balance has risen sharply, from -6.18% of the balance sheet total in 1993 to 39.43% in 2006. The abundance of liquidity they hold is also reflected in a sharp decline in refinancing resources, which represented only 0.19% of their combined balance sheet in 2006, compared with 60.55% in 1993.

It is important to note, however, that these overall trends conceal significant disparities - which can be seen in a more detailed analysis by country - as they are generally dependent on the situation of banks in Cameroon, a country with a market share of more than 50 percent of the CEMAC banking market[5] . However, there is a negative correlation between changes in bank liquidity and bank lending. When the latter decreases, liquidity tends to increase, and as a result, they have less recourse to central bank refinancing. But the truth is that the specificity of the Franc zone means that we are faced with a double overliquidity.

---

5 From 1993 to 2003, Cameroon accounted for an average of 49.76 percent of the total balance sheet of CEMAC banks; in 2006, Cameroonian banks accounted for 44.8 percent of the cumulative balance sheet of all banks in the zone. However, the market share of these banks has been declining in recent years.

The case we have just seen is in fact that of the excess liquidity of commercial banks vis-à-vis the BEAC and refers to a banking system that has a strong preference for liquidity and refuses to lend to economic agents.

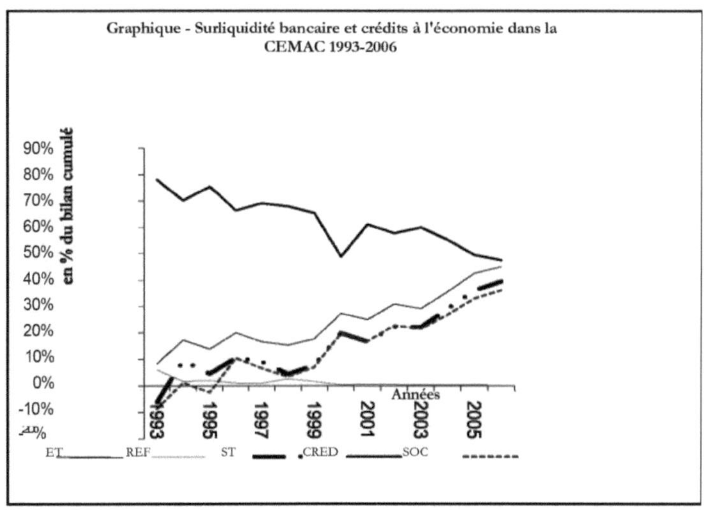

The second case, which is less visible, is that of the abundance of reserves held by the central banks vis-à-vis the outside world, which translates at the level of the zone into reserve surpluses far in excess of what is required for the guarantee given to the CFA franc by the French Treasury. It should be recalled that the issuance of currency in the zone is governed by the currency coverage ratio. This is clearly an intermediate objective of monetary policy, which operates, as in the monetarist rule, through the relationship of strict proportionality that links the monetary base, the money supply and the inflation rate. According to the IMF - International Financial Statistics, this rate was 94.65% in 2006. This is due to the increase in CEMAC's net foreign assets, which rose from 95.6 billion CFA francs in 1995 to 4,382.2 billion CFA francs in 2006, including 4,165.9 billion CFA francs deposited in the operating account.

Ultimately, the decline in credit to the economy in a context of abundant bank liquidity is undeniably a paradox, especially since the enormous economic potential of CEMAC contrasts sharply with the current level of economic and social development of the countries. In theoretical terms, this paradox stems from the lessons of the credit multiplier mechanism. However, the possession of prior resources is not sufficient for banks to engage in credit operations. As Lebourva (1962) so aptly points out, they first distribute credit and then worry about finding the necessary corresponding reserves. As we shall see, their behaviour as firms plays a key role in the supply of credit and greatly determines their liquidity position.

III- Determinants of excess bank liquidity in the CEMAC zone

Two main factors explain this excess liquidity: growing uncertainty in the subregion and financial liberalization.

3.1 .1 Growing uncertainty in the subregion

Indeed, factors related to uncertainty have increased banks' sensitivity to the risk of customer default and generated a strong preference for liquidity on their part. It will be recalled that the problem of excess bank liquidity in CEMAC emerged just after the devaluation of the CFA franc in January 1994, particularly with the sharp increase in the balance of transactions with customers of all commercial banks. This increased by more than 40 percent between December 1993 and the end of March 1996. Two main explanations for this were put forward.

The first was related to devaluation: this would have put an end to speculation and encouraged the massive repatriation of speculative capital placed outside the BEAC issuing zone. Since, some time earlier, capital flight had accelerated in the CEMAC zone, so much so that in 1991, for example, 50% of the banknotes issued by the BEAC had left the zone. By 1992, this proportion had risen to 60%, so that in the first half of 1993, capital flight in the entire franc zone reached 270 billion CFA francs, or nearly 15% of the money supply. As a result, the Banque de France decided in August 1993 to stop redeeming CFA franc banknotes, and the BEAC and BCEAO in turn decided to stop redeeming each other's bills. According to this explanation, these decisions had a positive impact on the banks' resources, as many clients opened bank accounts from that time on, so that they could make their transfers by law.

The second was linked to the deterioration of the economic situation and the absence of projects eligible for bank financing - so-called bankable projects. Indeed, the economies of CEMAC, like those of the rest of sub-Saharan Africa, had benefited from a significant improvement in terms of trade between 1973 and 1979. But with the second oil shock of 1979-1980 and the recession in the industrial countries, they experienced a sharp deterioration in their terms of trade (nearly 12 percent), which reached an unprecedented level from 1985 onward, with a decline of nearly 50 percent. Thus, by the end of 1992, cumulative declines amounted to 61% for oil, 73% for cocoa, 78% for coffee, 3% for cotton and 4% for wood. In short, the fall and growing instability of world commodity prices have caused a profound deterioration in their economic and financial situation.

As a result, Sub-Saharan African countries as a whole experienced a very negative evolution of real GDP growth and the overall fiscal balance. The latter rose from - 4.45 percent to 8.15 percent of GDP on average between 1986 and 1993. Over the same period, their external debt rose from 54.85% to 74.25% of GDP. All this resulted in a drying up of capital inflows into CEMAC, which fell from 637.5 to 353.9 billion CFA francs between 1985 and 1992.

However, this analysis, interesting as it may be, is not very credible today. If the devaluation led to an increase in bank liquidity, and the poor economic situation to a lack of bankable projects, this can no longer be the case today, since the macroeconomic framework in CEMAC has improved relatively in the meantime. In fact, it has not been noticed that the poor economic performance has led to a deterioration in the business environment, to the point where it has become one of the worst in the world, and has been denounced by many studies, such as the OECD (2007) studies on the economic outlook for Africa. According to the World Bank's World Business Environment Report 2007, the laws on collateral and bankruptcy are not conducive to credit development in Central Africa. In addition, judicial systems are characterized by inefficiencies in the resolution of commercial disputes, including a very high number of proceedings and very long settlement times. Not only are legal decisions slow to be made and difficult to enforce, but they are also often tainted by irregularities. These systems therefore do not provide sufficient incentives to encourage the development of financial contracts of any kind. The above-mentioned report shows that the law index of creditors and borrowers is below the average value (5).

In addition, as many studies point out (Wamba and Tchambe-Djiné (2002), Reinhart and Tokatlidis (2003), Chouchane-Verdier (2004), etc.), the information system is not conducive to credit decisions. There are no publicly managed databases that can collect information on the creditworthiness of borrowers, so the number of people with up-to-date information on their repayment history, outstanding debts, or outstanding credits is small. There is not even a credit bureau, private company, or non-profit organization that maintains a database of borrowers' creditworthiness and facilitates the exchange of credit information.

As a result, this radical uncertainty, in the words of Hugon (2007), makes risk non-probabilizable and increases banks' reluctance to lend. This translates into short-termist behavior, consisting not in making trade-offs between risk and profitability, but in choosing the short term and liquidity, which guarantee the greatest number of possible options in relation to the irreversibility of medium- or long-term credits. For this reason, it is noticeable that treasury operations are increasing, and represent the largest component of banks' cumulative assets (45% in 2006, for example). The same is true of interbank assets (40.45% of the cumulative balance sheet, with an amount of CFA francs 1,744 billion), which are constantly increasing (19.88% in 2006), whereas interbank resources are constantly decreasing and finally represent only a small proportion of their cumulative balance sheet (5.53%, with an amount of 238 billion). For example, in 2006, the total interbank balance was $1,506 billion, compared with $1,361 billion in 2005.

In addition, overnight and forward transactions are on the rise and consist mainly of investments at the BEAC (225 billion out of a total of 605 billion). The breakdown of loans to the economy according to their duration (table 4) completes these illustrations. Short-term loans accounted for an average of 69.37% of total loans to the economy between 1997 and 2006, as they are less risky than other forms of credit - around 30% - characterized by longer maturities.

Table 3: Breakdown of loans to the economy in the CEMAC (in millions of CFA francs)

Types of credit	1997	1998	1999	2000	20001	2002	2003	2004	2005	2006	Average share
CT	750893	841309	929666	1027031	1107865	1124112	1153781	1115358	1238984	1176091	69.37%
MT	251945	309228	292243	321426	348506	425556	474131	491969	553561	681498	27.51%
LT	42976	41092	41242	46757	43838	43515	45980	42980	57155	64664	3.12%
Total	1045814	1191629	1263151	1395214	1500209	1593183	1673892	1650307	1849700	1922253	100%

Source: BEAC 2006 p.64

Moreover, the financial difficulties encountered by the States have led to a spectacular decline in the two main components of bank activity, namely loans and deposits. Moreover, the fact that the public authorities wanted to make money an instrument of development resulted in a vast stateization of the banking systems, which led to a wide distribution of credit to public and non-public enterprises, with a high proportion of loans of convenience generally granted under political pressure (Guillaumont and Guillaumont-Jeanneney, 1993). It has also resulted in a systematic tendency to underestimate the probability of credit shocks, resulting from the default of one or more major borrowers. This tendency, which can be described as disaster myopia, in the language of Guttentag and Herring (1986), gave rise to this serious crisis.

According to the theory of disaster myopia, the credit crisis that results from disaster blindness is generally brutal and leads to a reversal of the banks' behaviour. This means that the blindness may be followed by a generalized mistrust of borrowers' solvency, so that banks may be led to drastically ration the quantity of credit granted, a behaviour that has been well known since the work of Hodgman (1960), Freimer and Gordon (1969) or Jaffee and Modigliani (1969), or even the relatively more recent work of Stiglitz and Weiss (1981).

More concretely, it has been noted that after the crisis, they adopted an excessively cautious attitude towards new credit operations. As a result, they have accumulated cash surpluses and increased their investments abroad. In addition, there is an increased preference for foreign companies and multinationals as clients - for which the risk is assumed to be low or even zero - compared to domestic SMEs, which have many weaknesses - family structure, lack of accounting, insufficient equity, information asymmetry, etc. - and are therefore more sensitive to risk. This greater sensitivity to risk was well illustrated in Cameroon, where Citibank financed the extension and modernization of the Société Mobile Téléphone Network (MTN) network, for a total amount of 23 billion CFA francs, repayable over seven years. In the same vein, the Société Générale des Banques au Cameroun (SGBC) granted a loan of 29 billion CFA francs to the Société Orange, for the same term. Very recently, in June 2007, a consortium of Cameroonian banks made up of SGBC, BICEC, Standard Chartered Bank Cameroon and Citibank Cameroon granted a loan of 44.5 billion CFA francs to MTN. It was noted that these credit operations were favored by the fact that they presented a very low or even zero risk, since MTN, for example, is a company that operates in the field of mobile telephony and benefits from the fashion effect, which allows it to achieve very high sales figures. This increased sensitivity to the risk of customer default has led to a reduction in the volume of credit and thus an increase in their liquid resources.

But this behavior alone does not explain their excess liquidity; it interacts with other factors, mostly related to changes brought about by financial liberalization.

III.2 Financial liberalization

Indeed, after the severe economic and financial crisis of the 1980s, most African countries south of the Sahara were led to implement neoliberal-inspired policies, through structural adjustment programs and financial liberalization policies. Widely advocated by McKinnon (1973) and Shaw (1973), these policies condemn government intervention in capital markets and advocate financial and banking reforms. In CEMAC, these reforms focused on monetary and savings policy instruments on the one hand, and on the institutional framework and financial institutions on the other (Avom and Eyeffa Ekomo, 2007). Their implementation has led to significant changes in the banking system[6] , changes that also explain the current excess liquidity of banks. Two changes can be mentioned for illustrative purposes only.

The first is related to the reorganization of banks. As a result of reforms, the financial structure of banks has improved considerably. For 2006, the rating system developed by COBAC (SYSCO system) to assess the financial situation of institutions shows that they are generally in good health; four banks were rated 1 (solid financial situation), 22 were rated 2 (good financial situation), three were rated 3 (fragile financial situation) and three others were rated 4 (critical financial situation). The strengthening of their financial structure has increased their credibility, particularly with depositors, who are by nature very sensitive to problems of illiquidity and insolvency. Indeed, the basic solvency ratio of the main banking networks in CEMAC reached 17.38% during the year, whereas the standard set by COBAC is 8%. In addition, adjusted net equity amounted to 169 billion compared to 149 billion in 2005, representing a solvency ratio of 13.43%. Book equity also increased to 338 billion, compared with 302 billion in 2005, i.e. a growth rate of 12.04%. The ratio of equity and permanent resources thus far exceeded the minimum level of 50%, reaching an average rate of 99.59% as of December 31, 2006. Moreover, as Table 4 shows, the banks' activity has been increasing every year, but with varying rates by country.

Table 4: Microeconomic Activities and Performance of CEMAC Banks

Years	2000	2001	2002	2003	2004	2005	2006
Net banking income (in millions of FCFA)	189216	208906	235687	244136	268030	284206	314414
Net results (in millions of FCFA)	48291	41232	38480	36082	49897	61944	73306
Profitability ratio (in %)	20.06	14.13	12.36	10.6	13.01	14.93	16.20
Efficiency ratio (in %)	1.88	1.76	1.37	1.29	1.61	1.64	1.70
Doubtful debts/accumulated balance sheet (in %)	5.67	6.77	6.73	7.25	6.99	5.98	5.11
Loans/cumulative balance sheet (in %)	48.81	61.02	57.70	59.88	55.31	49.47	47.53
Deposits/accumulated	63.76	72.18	74.22	74.87	76.11	77.37	78.87

---

6 This represents the bulk of financial assets in the CEMAC (see IMF, 2007).

balance sheet (in %)						
Rate of increase of the cumulative balance sheet (in %)	-8.39	19.52	-0.32	10.82	21.53	14.17

Source: COBAC annual reports 2004, 2005, 2006

Their combined balance sheet grew by 14.56% to CFAF 4,311 billion in 2006. This growth was accompanied by a restoration of profitability, so that their net profit amounted to 73.8 billion, an increase of 12.4% compared to their 2005 performance (61.9 billion). This profit, which represented more than 45% of their capitalization, is not the result of their traditional activity, since, thanks to financial liberalization, they have diversified their service offering and increased their fee-generating activities.

The second change concerns financial innovations, both in terms of new financial technologies - the electronification of money flows, the application of computers to banking and financial market transactions - and in terms of new financial assets. Innovations in financial products have focused on microfinance. In recent years, the Central African subregion has witnessed a very strong expansion of microcredit, particularly in urban centers (Malo and Koyadondri, 2006). Official sources indicate that as of December 31, 2006, the number of active microfinance institutions (MFIs) stood at 783, of which 679 had obtained COBAC approval. According to some, this expansion has led to competition in the banking market and an increase in banks' idle liquidity due to loss of market share. But the truth is that it has not led to significant competition, as the share of deposits and loans from microfinance has remained small compared to that of traditional banks - about 5% of banking activities. Instead, it is process innovations that have had a remarkable impact on the financial situation of banks. The development of new financial technologies has allowed them to increase the services that can generate fees. One example is electronic payments. Many banks now offer their customers bank cards affiliated with the international Visa network. These cards allow a large proportion of their customers to withdraw cash from ATMs and make payments at certain merchants. Some of them also offer E-banking or Internet banking services; those that have not yet introduced these technologies in their organization are working on it. These new services have led to the introduction of electronic clearing between credit institutions and the possibility of making bank cards interchangeable at national and international levels, as the financial stakes are so high. In the same vein, in September 2007, the Automated Large Value Transfer System (SYGMA) was set up to ensure the transfer of large sums of money between CEMAC banks in real time. A remote clearing system in Central Africa (SYSTAC) has also been made operational, and the interbank electronic payment system is scheduled to go into operation with the Central African Electronic Payments Office, which will lead to the introduction of a single bank card common to all credit institutions. A regional committee for the standardization of all these innovations has been set up - CORENOFI - because they appear to be necessary in the context of globalization and the acceleration of technological innovations, and above all, they are crucial to the profitability of banks.

In fact, they make it possible to increase net banking income without necessarily carrying out credit operations, in an environment that is moreover characterized by great uncertainty, since in return for all these new services, the clientele must pay the banks several commissions: on the subscription of a card, on each cash withdrawal operation, on each account consultation, as a contribution linked to the holding of the card, etc. Under these conditions, not only do their liquidities swell due to these various commissions, but they also become idle. In addition, as the OECD (2007) points out, liberalization has not led to genuine competition that would have lowered the cost of financial services. On the other hand, it has exacerbated the freedom of institutions to set their own prices, since they currently charge for all their services. Thus, they make various deductions from their clients' accounts, such as mail charges - about CFAF 1,580 - or the monthly management fee - about CFAF 2,500, etc.

In this chapter, we have just seen the economic and financial situation of the zone as well as the factors that can explain the excess liquidity of banks. In the next chapter, we will present the theoretical foundations and the literature on the relationship between bank excess liquidity and the financing of the economy.

CHAPTER II: THEORETICAL FOUNDATIONS AND REVIEWS OF THE LITERATURE ON THE RELATIONSHIP BETWEEN EXCESS BANK LIQUIDITY AND ECONOMIC FINANCING

Introduction

In the CEMAC, banks prefer to build up idle cash balances given the risks associated with bank financing mentioned in the previous chapter. Indeed, banks prefer to take advantage of a rent situation rather than take the risk of financing productive activities and, when they do finance them, the level of interest rates is such that only the tertiary sector benefits. The increase in the issuance of public debt securities, which constitutes a new opportunity for rent, only accentuates this trend.

The overliquidity of the banking system is neither favourable to banking intermediaries, who retain idle financing capacity, nor to private investors, who are in dire need of financing. In other words, it is the economy of the zone that will be hampered if the trend is not reversed. To better understand the problem of excess bank liquidity on the financing of the economy, it is important to first look at the concepts of excess liquidity and financing of the economy and then review the theoretical foundations of its relationship with the financing of the economy as well as the related economic literature.

1- Bank overliquidity

Mastering the concept of excess bank liquidity requires defining it and determining its causes.

1.1 Definition of excess bank liquidity

The concept of bank liquidity has two dimensions that must be distinguished. In order to understand which of the liquidities is relevant to our study in the WAEMU banking system, it is essential to analyze the aspects of this concept and to highlight the links that may exist between them.

With the financial crisis that started in the United States, many studies have been done on the issue of bank liquidity. In the most extensive literature, there are two main interpretations of bank liquidity. These include "market liquidity" and "funding liquidity". However, these two concepts are very closely related.

❖ Market liquidity

The concept of market liquidity has been at the heart of the crisis where all compartments of the financial markets have been affected. Before addressing the latter, it is appropriate to first define the liquidity of a financial asset. In reality, it refers to the speed with which an asset can be exchanged for money without loss of value. In other words, it refers to the ability of the market to absorb transactions on a given volume of assets or securities without significant effect on their prices. The degree of liquidity can be assessed using three criteria[6] :

S The width of the bid-ask spread which measures the transaction costs of holding the asset;

S The depth of the market which refers to the volume of transactions that can be immediately executed without a price shift at the best limit;

S The resilience of the market, i.e. the speed with which prices return to their equilibrium level following a random shock in the flow of transactions.

In addition to this definition, market liquidity is used in the banking literature to refer to the ability of a bank to trade a non-monetary asset quickly, without delay and without loss of capital, against ultimate liquidity, which is par excellence the Central Bank's money. This second definition focuses instead on the ability of the holder of the asset to dispose of it at a decent price. The underlying idea is that the bank may, at some point, need central bank money for one reason or another. However, it turns out that not all of its assets have the same degree of liquidity and that the market on which these assets are traded may be more or less liquid depending on the circumstances. Market liquidity is therefore a relative concept, as a bank may not be

---

6 BERVAS, 2006

able to obtain base money given the nature of the assets it holds and/or the state of market liquidity. In this paper, the term "market liquidity" will be used in the latter sense. In contrast, market liquidity is not the focus of this study, but neither can we dispense with this concept because of the link between the two meanings of bank liquidity.

❖ Financing liquidity

Funding liquidity refers to the liquidity needed to meet short-term withdrawal requests from counterparties or to cover their operations[7] . According to this definition, a banking institution is said to be liquid if it has sufficient liquidity, or the ability to mobilize it quickly, to cover its liabilities according to their maturity during a given period, often less than three months. It is linked to the particularity of the banking industry. This particularity is explained by its exposure to transformation risk. In fact, banks often provide long-term financing by mobilizing short and/or medium-term resources. In doing so, they take the risk of exposing themselves to unexpected withdrawal requests from their clientele. The holding of a certain amount of liquidity by a bank is therefore necessary to face the above-mentioned risk. The problem is that holding a certain amount of liquidity may, under certain circumstances, be inconsistent with the banks' profitability objective. Thus, we speak of "wasted liquidity" when a banking institution holds a quantity of liquidity beyond what is necessary to cover the operations of its customers and without strategic motivation. The management of liquidity is thus made delicate since it leads to an ambivalence between the need for prudence and the objective of profitability.

This phenomenon is all the more delicate because a banking panic, a rush following the failure or illiquidity of a bank, can have repercussions on the entire financial system and call into question financial stability. Thus, prudential regulation, particularly with respect to bank liquidity management, has been necessary to safeguard the financial system from excessive risk-taking by any one bank. Nevertheless, prudential arrangements, however necessary, do not reduce bank liquidity risk to zero. This is the result, on the one hand, of the uncertainty that reigns in the markets, an uncertainty that accentuates the links between the two dimensions of liquidity and that reveals the relative nature of the liquidity of an asset and, on the other hand, of the asymmetry of information between the legislator and the banker. The recurrence of banking and financial crises can only validate this assertion.

I.2 The causes of excess bank liquidity in the CEMAC zone

Prudential rules require all banks to hold a certain amount of liquidity, but excess liquidity can be counterproductive. However, the reasons for excessive liquidity holding have become a concern for some political authorities in the Union, so there is an urgent need to know the causes of this phenomenon.

In theory, the excess liquidity of CEMAC banks can be explained by three factors: constraints related to the parity of the CFA franc, capital inflows, and high interest rates.

❖ **Constraints related to the parity of the CFA franc**

The excess liquidity in the Union's banks began after the devaluation of the CFA franc in 1994. The devaluation allowed the CEMAC to initiate a series of measures and reforms to accompany a shock, especially following the failure of structural adjustment policies. The internal and external stability of the value of the currency is the major concern of the monetary authorities, and the constitution of foreign exchange reserves has become a primary objective of monetary policy. To achieve this objective, the political authorities grant facilities to encourage outward-oriented activities that earn foreign exchange. On the other hand, the monetary authorities impose strong constraints, obliging commercial banks to repatriate their foreign currency if it is too large abroad. These constraints have resulted in a preference for banks to finance the short and medium term in the tertiary sector, particularly trade, while the share of credit granted to enterprises and inward-oriented productive sectors is very limited.

❖ **Constraints on capital inflows**

The measures implemented in the monetary system have also resulted in a significant influx of capital. Since the banking system is conducive to the financing of outward-oriented enterprises (agricultural, commercial and mining), these have developed and contributed to a greater or lesser extent to the overall liquidity of the zone through foreign trade and depending on the international environment (commodity prices and the prices of the currencies in which these commodities are quoted). In addition, remittances from emigrants constitute an important part of capital inflows. These transfers, as important as they are, are difficult to quantify because of the large number of informal money transfer networks. They occupy an increasingly important place in the balance of payments of a number of countries. As a result, they are attracting the interest of authorities and banks. In addition to these factors, the role played by official development assistance and by the cancellation of the debt of certain countries following the Heavily Indebted Poor Countries initiative should also be highlighted.

Table 5: Evolution of the main balances of the CEMAC balance of payments (in billions of CFAF)

YEARS	2003	2004	2005	2006	2007	2008	2009	2010	2011
Trade balance	3309,5	5454,9	8321,2	9070,4	8944,8	12022, 2	5221,0	8708,1	11708, 6
Balance of Services	2203,5	-2557,3	-2704,6	-3436,3	-3415,1	-4089,7	-3755,8	-5093,8	-5500,2
Current transfers balance	65,7	119,2	228,2	184,2	373,7	334,3	367,3	299,6	317,3
Balance of capital and financial operations	523,8	147,1	-182,3	-72,6	294,3	607,0	1123,6	1820,1	1018,8
overall balance	-583,8	68,8	1012,8	1300,4	772,9	2057,3	-1119,8	-31,4	832,3

Source: constructed from CEMAC data, March 2011

A number of observations can be made about the balance of payments (Table 6). First, the overall balance is almost always in surplus (except in 2003, 2009 and 2010). This means that capital inflows exceed outflows, which translates into a systematic increase in the overall liquidity of the CEMAC. The surplus in this balance in 2006 is essentially attributable to debt cancellation. Second, the trade balance and the financial transactions and current transfers balances are also mostly in surplus. The surplus in these balances explains the surplus in the overall account. However, it is in the balance of services that the Union has a chronic deficit.

❖ **Interest rate constraints.**

The high level of interest rates hinders the financing of activity. It does not in itself explain the excess liquidity in the Union's banking system, but it is a block to recycling this excess liquidity for productive purposes. This increase excludes some borrowers from the formal financing circuit, creating a problem of adverse selection. In addition, it is an obstacle to the development of activities for both companies and the banks themselves. Indeed, the high level of interest rates can lead to an increase in the proportion of defaulted loans. The resulting increase in default risks could lead to an increase in the probability of financial crises. Four main reasons are often given for the high interest rates and the resulting under-financing of the economy:

- the significant risk of borrower default,

- the lack of bankable projects,

- the lack of accounting standards and (4) the weakness of the judicial system.

Lower rates are necessary to encourage less risky borrowing that is favorable to business development and, by extension, to the banking system.

II- The notion of financing the economy

The financing of the economy can be understood as all the mechanisms through which economic agents resort to the capital held by other economic agents with financing capacities.

2.1 1 Types of financing of the economy

There are two types of funding, indirect funding and direct funding.

■ **Indirect funding:**

Indirect financing of economic activity implies that there is an economic agent who faces the link between the various economic agents. This is called financial intermediation. This intermediation is carried out by financial institutions (banks), which on the one hand collect savings from households, and on the other hand lend to companies the sums necessary to finance their activity. An economy that functions essentially through the intermediation role of banks is called a "**debt economy**.

- **Direct funding:**

Financial institutions charge borrowers for their financial intermediation services, which makes it more expensive for agents with financing deficits to obtain resources. This has the effect of making it more expensive for agents with financing deficits to obtain resources. These agents are therefore led to look for ways to avoid having to use these financial intermediaries. To do this, they will turn directly to economic agents with financing capacities. Companies, or the State, will therefore go through the financial markets by issuing investment securities that will be acquired directly by economic agents wishing to make their available savings grow. If an economy functions essentially thanks to the financial markets, we speak of a "**financial market economy**".

There are two types of capital markets:

- **The money market, which is by definition a short-term capital market where short-term securities are exchanged for cash**.

This market is reserved for institutional investors, exclusively banks and insurance companies, which lend capital to each other on a short-term basis. There is also a compartment where companies can issue commercial paper or invest surplus cash. This market allows participants to find sources of financing for needs related to short-term cash flow shortfalls. In the case where the financing need concerns a longer term, the agent with a financing deficit will turn to the financial market.

- **The financial market, which is by definition the long-term capital market**.

Securities are traded on this market. There are two compartments: the primary market on which newly issued securities are sold by agents with financing needs, and the secondary market (the stock exchange) on which these securities are traded between economic agents.

Overall, regardless of the type of financing chosen or the capital market considered, financing the economy presents a number of difficulties and risks.

2.2 2 Difficulties related to bank financing and risks

The main factors hindering bank financing in the countries of the zone are related to the business environment, the level of bank penetration and the distribution of credit in the various sectors.

❖ **Business environment challenges**:

The business climate is a major factor inhibiting the development of credit to investors. Indeed, the degree of economic uncertainty in the countries of a zone, accompanied by chronic socio-political instability, pushes banks to adopt a risk-averse behavior. This situation makes it costly to obtain information on borrowers and evaluate their projects, which is detrimental to business development and limits the ability to forecast and design reliable medium and long-term investment plans. In other words, the business climate has a negative impact on the demand for and distribution of bank credit.

In the same vein, the tax burden in some countries in the region is not conducive to the investment climate and is becoming a brake on the development of bank credit. Moreover, relations between banks and their clients are also deteriorated by the administrative burden in handling disputes, as well as the unsuitability of legal provisions and their application deemed unfair to the detriment of financial institutions.

The accumulation of payment arrears of the States prevents the obtaining of new credits because the repayment of the previous credits is not possible. In addition, the relatively high level of interest rates charged by banks does not allow companies to resort to bank credit, despite the efforts of the Central Bank.

The breakdown of credits is also a relevant factor that reinforces the inaccessibility of bank credits to companies. Indeed, long-term credits are almost insignificant compared to short-term credits. Moreover, the latter are oriented more towards the trade sector to the detriment of the primary and secondary sectors

❖ **Financing risks**:

The poor closing of project financing schemes by investors limits the development of bank credits, but there is also the insufficiency of equity contributions, the weakness of managerial capacity, the unreliable character of the financial statements produced, etc.

To overcome these difficulties, the BCEAO, as part of the implementation of the new money and credit policy rules, has set up a control instrument called the Rating Agreements. They are a tool for the a posteriori control of credits distributed by the banking system. With this instrument, the issuing institution leaves the banks with full responsibility for the loans they distribute. In return, it determines the bank claims that can be mobilized from the Central Bank, the objective being to encourage banks to hold sound assets and to constantly monitor the quality of their portfolio.

Having reviewed the concepts of excess liquidity and financing of the economy separately, it is now important to consider the theoretical underpinnings of the relationship between these two concepts.

III- Theoretical foundations of the relationship between bank liquidity and financing of the economy

The mechanism of the credit multiplier, although theoretically unsuited to the debt economy, is at the root of the conception that deposits make credits. Its starting point is the controversy over the money supply. Already raised in the nineteenth century, during the debate between the Banking School and the Currency School, this controversy continued and gave rise to the opposition between the credit multiplier and the credit divider. According to this mechanism, when the central bank increases the central bank money (monetary base), the commercial banks recover a fraction of it in the form of deposits and engage in lending the excess liquidity that does not earn them anything.

The credits granted in turn give rise to new deposits, which will be lent out again, and so on. Monetarists establish a mathematical link between the monetary base issued by the central bank and the money in circulation in the economy. If we consider the dynamic chains of deposits and loans, this mechanism shows that commercial banks have the capacity to create money at a multiple of the monetary base, from an exogenous increase in the monetary base. According to this mechanism, commercial banks can therefore only grant credit if they have excess liquidity, but the amount of which is perfectly determined by the central bank. They are therefore constrained by prior resources, and can only grant loans if they have resources at the outset.

In other words, an excess of liquidity on their balance sheet is logically sufficient for them to grant credit. From a bank's point of view, it is the idea that it is the customers' deposits that make credit operations possible that is so deeply rooted in people's minds that Levy-Garboua (1992) says that the teaching of macroeconomics, according to which credits make deposits, has lost its force, thus giving rise to an abundant literature.

IV- Literature review and empirical work

As for the relationship between bank liquidity and the financing of the economy in the CEMAC zone, very few studies have addressed this issue. We can cite in particular Fouda Owoundi (2009) in his article "bank overliquidity in the franc zone: how to explain the CEMAC paradox".

In this article, the author starts from the fact that the holding of a volume of liquidity by banks is theoretically justified by their mission of liquidity insurance. He notes that for the past fifteen years, banks in the Franc zone have held abundant liquidity that is much higher than what is necessary for this mission and, paradoxically, the credits granted to the economy have been decreasing. It therefore proposes an analysis of the determinants of this excess liquidity based on the case of the six CEMAC member countries. This analysis is supported by empirical tests using panel data of aggregated bank balance sheets and income statements for the period 1993-

2006. Following a series of tests, the analysis finds an interaction between several factors: the uncertainty linked to the sharp deterioration of the business climate, the memory effect of previous banking crises and the reinforcement of banks' reluctance, as well as the financial innovations brought about by financial liberalization.

Although the issue of bank liquidity is not yet the subject of an abundant literature in the sub-region, it is nevertheless of interest internationally. With this in mind, Soumaila Doumbia, in his article on *"Le sous financement des entreprises dans un contexte de surliquidité bancaire : le paradoxe de l'UEMOA"* (May 2009), identifies three main causes, namely constraints related to the defense of the parity of the CFA franc, capital inflows and high interest rates. In his article, he emphasizes the excess liquidity of banks in the WAEMU in a context of under-financing of the productive sector and SMEs. According to him, banks tend to overestimate the risk associated with the financing of a large proportion of firms, which results in insufficient loans vis-à-vis deposits and, therefore, in an increase in their liquidity beyond the necessary threshold. The author also points out that the excess liquidity of banks initially gave rise to idle deposits with the Central Bank before being recycled in part to finance sovereign debt. This phenomenon contributed to reducing the size of excess reserves without absorbing them entirely. In the end, the author stresses that the problem of excess liquidity has not been totally resolved and that the problem of financing the economy has simply changed in nature. However, the author limits his analysis to describing the problem. He does not seek to solve or at least to provide ideas for solving the problem of financing the economy through access to credit.

In the *Journal of International Economics 63 (2004)* Wai-Ming Ho examines the effectiveness of foreign exchange intervention in two countries and two different currencies in a general equilibrium model that allows for liquidity effects. He shows that both sterilizing and non-sterilizing intervention have a significant impact on the allocation of liquidity in international financial markets. His model shows that there are circumstances where the exchange rate response to intervention is paradoxical as indicated in the empirical literature.

Alberto Giovannini, in his article "*Monetary policy, liquidity, and foreign exchange markets*" in Journal of Monetary Economics 33 (1994), explores empirically the fluctuations in money demand resulting from financial markets. He shows that liquidity fluctuations in financial markets are reflected in interest rates and asset returns. He studies the effects of liquidity shocks in the financial and foreign exchange markets in Switzerland before 1988. He finally shows that liquidity shocks were an important determinant of ex ante foreign currency deposit returns to Swiss franc deposits.

Agénor and El Aynaoui worked on "Excess *liquidity, bank pricing rules, and monetary policy*", Journal of Banking & Finance (2009). Their paper studies the implications of excess bank liquidity on the effectiveness of monetary policy in a simple model with credit market imperfection. The demand for excess liquidity is determined by precautionary factors and the opportunity cost of holding liquidity. They show that excess liquidity can impart greater liquidity to the deposit rate following a monetary contraction and induce collateral requirements on borrowers; which in turn can lead to low premium risk and low lending rates. Finally, they show that asymmetric price behavior at the bank level under excess liquidity can hamper the effectiveness of monetary policy contraction through low inflation.

This chapter has allowed us to briefly review the economic literature on monetary policy through the interbank market and the role of the Central Bank in this market. In addition, a review of the literature on liquidity and its role in the financing of the economy has been made. Empirically, the main factors of excess bank liquidity in the CEMAC zone are reserve requirements, the lending rate, inflation, financial deepening and banks' net foreign assets. However, in accordance with our main research question, it is important to present the methodology that will allow us to analyze and interpret the empirical results.

CHAPTER III: METHODOLOGICAL FRAMEWORK OF THE STUDY AND EVOLUTION OF BANKING LIQUIDITY FACTORS IN THE CEMAC ZONE

Introduction

In this chapter we will see the different sections that will allow us to establish a brief description of our model. It will explain the choice of the model, present our variables and indicate our sources, and finally specify the model.

However, before presenting the theoretical framework on which our model is based, it seems appropriate to review the evolution of the factors of excess liquidity identified in the previous chapter.

1- Evolution of monetary aggregates, factors of excess bank liquidity

The aggregates of interest in this study are: financing of the economy, net foreign assets, bank reserves, money supply, lending rate and inflation.

1.1 Evolution of credits to the economy

The outstanding loans to the economy increased from 1593.183 billion in December 2002 to 3623.233 billion in December 2010, an increase of 127.42%, due to ordinary loans which increased by 1089.659 billion, the campaign loans also increased by 8.125 billion.

Overall, this evolution was reflected in the expansion of short-term and medium-term credits by 1097.784 billion (54.07%) and 867.239 billion (42.72%) respectively.

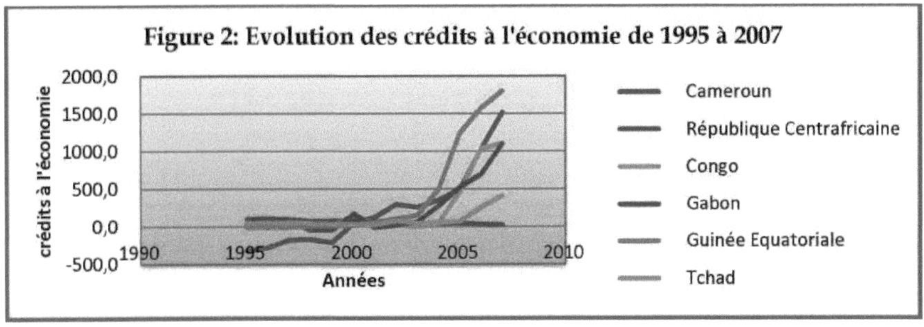

Figure 2: Evolution des crédits à l'économie de 1995 à 2007

Source: Constructed by the author from CEMAC 2011 data

The graph above shows that the structure of financing of the economy, as measured by the variable "credits to the economy", differs according to the economic weight of the country. Cameroon's structure of financing of the economy, through credits, is almost constant if we follow the trend from 2002 to 2006. However, there has been an increase in financing since 2006. In addition, this country, which accounts for 40% of the zone's GDP, has the highest level of financing, followed by Gabon, with the Central African Republic coming in last place.

1.2 Evolution of the Net External Assets

Net foreign assets of monetary institutions stood at \$288.483 billion in 2010, up \$7.019 billion from the end of December 2009[10] . This strengthening of the external position is mainly attributable to the mobilization of external resources in support of the economic and financial programs of the States. However, in our study we take into account the net external assets of banks and not of the Central Bank.

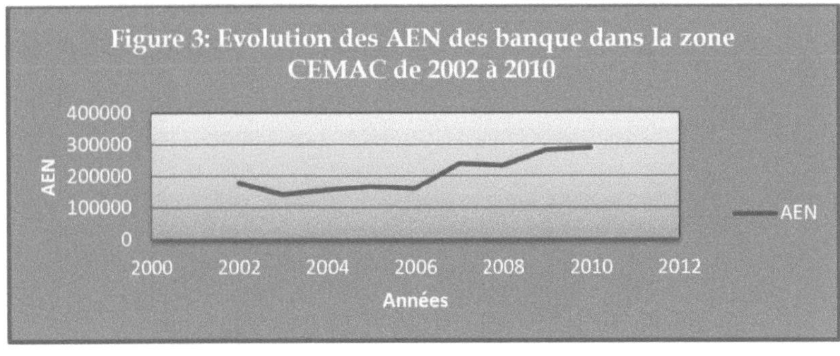

Figure 3: Evolution des AEN des banque dans la zone CEMAC de 2002 à 2010

---

10 CEMAC data 2011

Source: Constructed by the author from CEMAC 2011 data

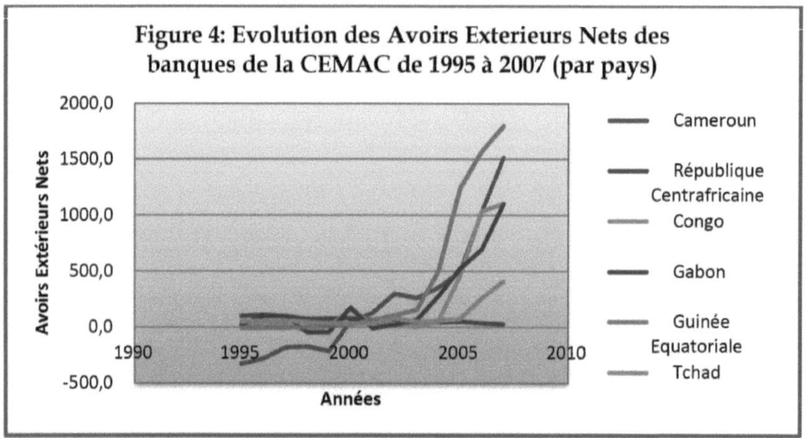

Source: Constructed by the author from CEMAC 2011 data

In terms of bank NEAs, Equatorial Guinea has been in first place since 2004, which can be explained by the country's high oil production, which constitutes foreign exchange earnings.

1.3 Evolution of bank reserves

The system of reserve requirements aims to strengthen the effectiveness of interest rates within the monetary management system of the Central Bank, influencing the liquidity of banks and their ability to grant credit. It allows to differentiate, by state, the coefficients of required reserves of banks and financial institutions.

When analyzing the evolution of required reserves and those actually constituted, it appears that the latter were on average largely in deficit in CEMAC for the year 2010. The only cases of surpluses were in January and June. Overall, there was a surplus of CFAF 2,288 million for a deficit of CFAF 8,056 million, i.e., a total deficit of CFAF 6,3768 million.

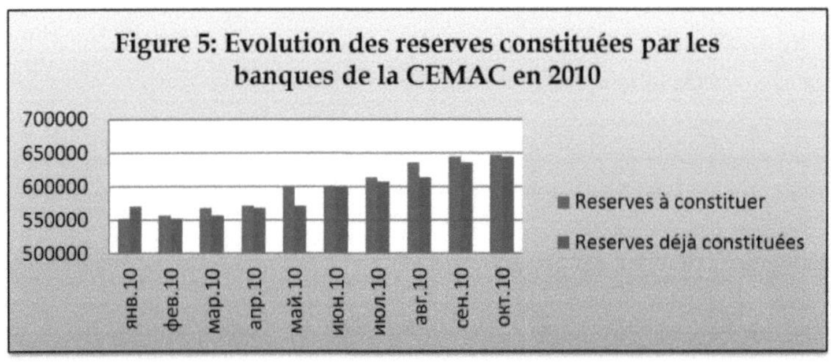

Figure 5: Evolution des reserves constituées par les banques de la CEMAC en 2010

Source: Constructed by the author from CEMAC 2011 data

1.4   Evolution of the money supply

It has increased since 1987 to reach 2921.6 billion in 2004, and stood at 4611.5 billion in 2007, an increase of 57.42%. This increase is attributable to the growth of net foreign assets, domestic credits and other net items, bank deposits and fiduciary circulation.

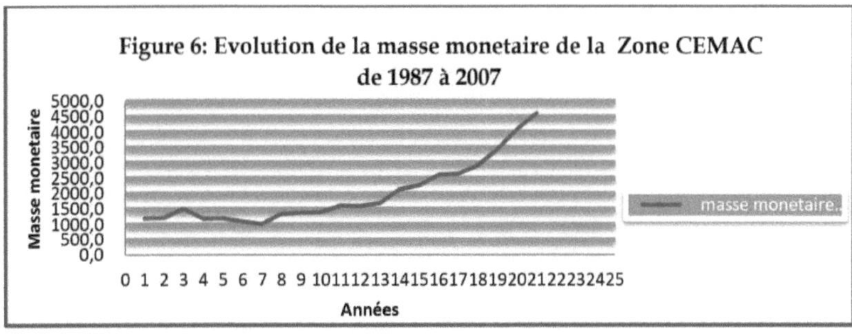

Figure 6: Evolution de la masse monetaire de la Zone CEMAC de 1987 à 2007

Source: Constructed by the author from CEMAC 2011 data

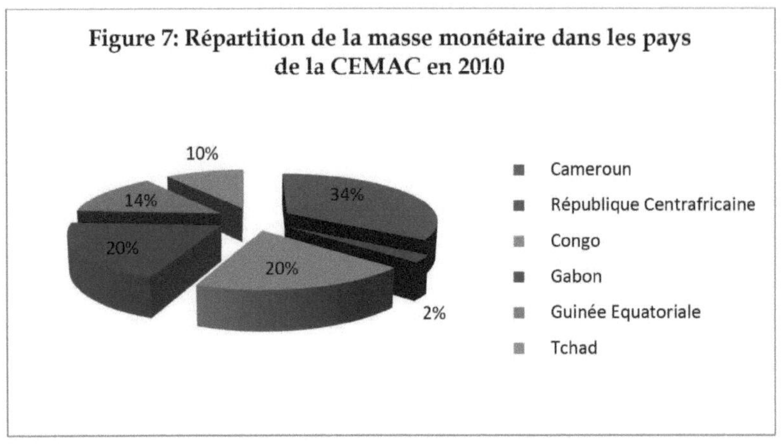

Source: Constructed by the author from CEMAC 2011 data

1.5 Evolution of lending rates

In our model, the lending rate represents the cost of credit. However, given the difficulty of obtaining aggregate data for this variable, we have taken a weighted average of the interest rate for CEMAC member countries. Based on this composition, we can say that the evolution of the lending rate has been up and down over the period from 1987 to 2007, with a peak in 1997, 1998 and 1999.

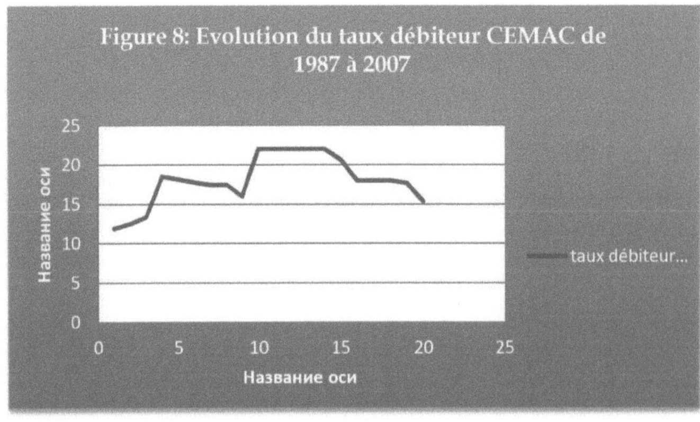

Source: Constructed by the author from CEMAC 2011 data

1.6 Inflation trends in the CEMAC zone

Inflation in the CEMAC zone has evolved in a sawtooth pattern from 1987 to 2007 with a peak in 1994. This sawtooth evolution is most noticeable between 2000 and 2010. During this period, the level of inflation rose from 1.37 to 4.30 in 2001. This rate will then fall to 0.63 in 2004 and rise to 5.25 in 2006 to settle at 1.2 in 2010.

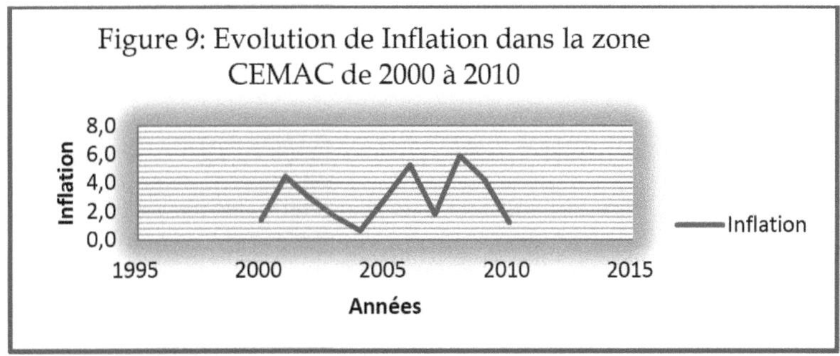

Source: Constructed by the author from CEMAC 2011 data

Finally, an analysis of the evolution of monetary aggregates reveals a consolidation of the net foreign assets of monetary institutions and an intensification of the increase in money supply, under the effect of an increase in domestic credit following a rise in the number of loans granted in member states which have recorded a recovery in their economic activity after several years of stagnation.

In the light of this separate evolution of these different monetary aggregates, this report aims to observe the relationship that these different components may have with each other, more specifically, the relationship between the financing of the economy in the sub-region and other factors. To achieve this, we will use an econometric model that is important to present.

1.7 Econometric approach to the relationship between bank liquidity and economic financing

Referring to the analyses of the evolution of the aggregates used in our model in the previous section, the objective of this section is to present the methodology necessary to conduct our econometric approach.

In this section we will look at the different sections that will allow us to establish a brief description of our model. It will explain the choice of the model, present our variables and indicate our sources, and finally specify the model.

After this introductory work, we will use panel data analysis in order to have more information leading to a greater precision of the estimates. For each of the panel data models, we will choose three variants: a model without effects, a fixed effects model and a random effects model that we will estimate with the STATA11 software. We will perform specification tests at the 5% threshold for each of the three models in order to choose, among the three variants, the one that best suits our data. From an econometric point of view, this amounts to testing the equality of the coefficients of the model studied in the individual dimension. Next, we will look at the individual effects models.

The application will be made on a file that includes data for the six (6) CEMAC countries and over 20 years.

II.1 Model selection, data source and variables

Our study is inspired by Demirgüç-Kunt & Huizinga (1999). It is a linear model that we adapt to the problem of bank financing of the economy.

The empirical analysis of the determinants of bank profitability proposed by Demirguç-Kunt and Huizinga (1999) is certainly the most important. It concerns 80 developed and developing countries, over the period 1989 to 1995. They show a positive correlation between bank capitalization and profitability, as well as a negative relationship between the latter and the reserves built up by the banks.

Our sample will be constructed in such a way as to produce a cross-sectional and temporal panel covering a period of twenty years (1987-2007) and the six CEMAC countries, namely Cameroon, Congo, Gabon, Equatorial Guinea, Central African Republic and Chad.

Among the exogenous variables, we have selected those that seem to us to correspond best to the situation of the banking systems in the zone. For the banking structure variables, we have credits to the economy (CE), net foreign assets of banks (AEN), bank reserves (RE) and bank lending rates (ID).

We have chosen two macroeconomic variables. First, there is the inflation rate (INFL), which is actually the price index that measures the evolution of prices. And finally, the financial depth (M2/GDP), which measures the depth of the financial market and can tell us something about banking. It is the ratio of money supply to GDP.

Following Demirgüç-Kunt & Huizinga (1999), our basic econometric model is of the following form:

$$CE_{nt} = \alpha_n + \beta_{1nt}RE_{nt} + \beta_{2nt}AEN_{nt} + \beta_{3nt}INFL_{nt} + \beta_{4nt}ID_{nt} + \beta_{5nt}(\frac{M2}{PIB})_{nt} + \varepsilon_{nt} \quad (1)$$

With $n \rightarrow 1$ *to N* (*N*= {*Cameroon*, Congo, Gabon, Equatorial Guinea, Central African Republic, and Chad}) and $t \rightarrow$ *1987 to 2007*; CE_{nt} the explained; and a_n the constant; RE_{nt}, AEN_{nt}, $INFL_{nt}$, ID_{nt}, $(M2/GDP)_{nt}$ are the explanatory variables; β_n the coefficients and e_{nt} the white noise residuals.

The various data on these values come mainly from the 2011 BEAC database. To this we add the World Development Indicators 2008.

The model, as well as the evolution of the monetary aggregates thus presented, it is important to present the results obtained.

CHAPTER V: PRESENTATION, INTERPRETATION AND DISCUSSION OF RESULTS

Introduction

In line with the research problem and the objectives of this monograph, this chapter will present an overview of the relationship between excess bank liquidity and the financing of the economy in the CEMAC sub-region using panel data on the economies of the sub-region from 1987 to 2007. The methodology used to obtain the results below is that of Demirgüç-Kunt & Huizinga (1999). The use of panel data requires procedures and tests of the results obtained.

1- Test procedures and results

If we consider model **(1)**, then several configurations are possible: 1. The N constants a_n and the N parameter vectors β_η are identical: $a_n = a;\ \beta_\eta = \beta\ V\ \mathrm{Ie} \in [7;N]$. We then call the panel a homogeneous panel.

2. The N constants a_n and the N parameter vectors β_η are different for each individual. So we have N different models, we reject the panel structure.

3. The N constants a_n are identical, $a_n = a\ V\ i \in [7;N]$; while the parameter vectors β_η differ across individuals. In this case, all the coefficients of the model, except the constants, are different for each individual. We thus have N different models.

4. The N parameter vectors β_η are identical, $\beta_\eta = \beta\ V\ i \in [7;N]$; while the constants a_n differ across individuals. We obtain a model with individual effects. In order to discriminate between these different configurations and to ensure that the panel structure is well-founded, it is necessary to adopt a procedure for testing nested homogeneity, presented by Hsiao (1986).

> **Specification Test Results**

First of all, we observe that the panel is non-cylindrical (unbalanced), that is to say that it does not have the same number of points in the temporal dimension for all individuals. Indeed, starting from the distribution N=6 and T= 21, i.e. 126 observations, we note only 99, i.e. a gap of 27. This gap is explained by the fact that the variable net external assets is not available for the first five years for five countries. The specification in our study will begin by testing the significance of the group effect. To do this, we will calculate the Fisher statistic under the following assumptions.

Ho: $\alpha_1 = \alpha_2 = \alpha_3 = \ldots \alpha_N$

$H_1 : \exists 1\ \alpha_i \neq$ *of the others*

The calculation of the Fisher statistic given by :

$$F(n-1)(nt-k-1) = \frac{(R^2_{lsd} - R^2_{pooled})/(n-1)}{(1 - R^2_{lsd})/(nt-k-1)}$$

AN : F(5,88) = 3.2370 > P - value (0.9936), so we reject the null hypothesis

> **Model Estimation**

In this part, we will first estimate the fixed-effect model and then the random-effect model and finally choose which one to use.

> **Fixed effects model**

Here we make the assumption that the individual effects a_n are represented by constants (hence the name fixed effects model). We will determine the general form of the estimators of the parameters α_n and β_n in this fixed effects model. Consider model (1) under hypothesis H0: $Y_{nt} = \alpha_n + \beta'x_{nt} + \varepsilon_{nt}$ V∈ i [*1;N]*

The calculations made by the software stata.11, gives :

F test that all u_i=0: F (5, 88) =106   .83Prob   > F =

0.0000

Since the probability of rejection is zero, we accept the H0 hypothesis, thus confirming the presence of fixed effects.

> **Random effects model**

Here we need to test the hypothesis of no effects against the hypothesis of random effects.

The results obtained by the software show that :

Wald chi2(5)   =121   .47 andProb   > chi2 =0 .0000

Since the probability of rejection is zero, we accept the hypothesis H1 of the presence of random effects.

> **Choice of the model to be retained**

The choice of our model was made on the basis of the Breusch and Pagan random effect test which gives a chi2(1) = 395.73 (positive), thus confirming the random effect model which will therefore be retained.

II-Interpretation of results

The random effects model shows that the model is globally significant. The explanatory variables that are significant are two (2): reserves and net foreign assets.

Table: Presentation of variable estimates

Varia ble	Coef	Std. Err	z	P>/z/	95% Conf. Interval
RE	2.673591	.300014 1	8.91	0.000	2.085574 3.261608
NEA	-.2947949	.0765424	-3.85	0.000	-.4448154 -.1447745

Source: made by the author from stata.11 results

Reserves: their coefficient is positive (β_2= 2.673591), which means that an increase of 1% in the financing of the economy, i.e. credits to the economy, is due to an increase of about 2.7% in reserves, thus confirming hypothesis H1. This result is perfectly predictable in the hypotheses, insofar as economic theory maintains that it is the deposits that make the credits. In other words, since reserves are made up of deposits and cash, the increase in deposits will result in additional liquidity that allows for the financing of firms and individuals through loans.

Net foreign assets: their coefficient is negative and is worth $\beta=-.2947949$, this result is also predictable, since the foreign assets of banks are repatriated if the amount is surplus by the BEAC. Thus, we can say that a 1% increase in credits to the economy is due to a 0.30% decrease in net foreign assets, thus confirming hypothesis H2.

Finally, the econometric analysis of our variable-effects model allows us to conclude that the excess liquidity of banks in the CEMAC zone, through reserve requirements and net foreign assets, does indeed affect the financing of the economy. However, the effects differ according to the variables. While the increase in bank reserves leads to an increase in loans granted to finance the economy, the increase in net foreign assets reduces them.

General conclusion and recommendations

At the end of our study, we understand that the analysis of the link between bank financing of the economy and bank liquidity is essential to understand the factors on which it would be necessary to act in order to solve the problem of financing the States of the Union.

In a context of constant change and marked by numerous upheavals that have an impact on the functioning of economies at the international level on the one hand and on market integration on the other, the permanent adaptation of CEMAC monetary authorities and their instruments is not always easy.

The zone's monetary authorities, by introducing reforms to correct excess liquidity, are at the same time attempting to resolve the recurring issue of bank financing for the economies of CEMAC member countries.

Moreover, the economic literature on the issue of bank liquidity is abundant, but as far as CEMAC is concerned, the question of bank financing, accompanied paradoxically by excess liquidity in the system, remains unanswered for the time being. The financing of the economy within the zone faces enormous difficulties related to access to bank credit and difficulties related to the business environment.

Concerned about the magnitude of the phenomenon and the enormous financing needs, the Heads of State of CEMAC met within the framework of the consultations on the banking financing of the economy in the States of the zone. The objective of these consultations is to provide a framework for the various actors involved in the financial sector, enabling them to take stock of the state of bank financing of the economy in the CEMAC countries and to find appropriate solutions to the difficulties of accessing financing for agents.

Our investigation, which is based on the Demirgüç-Kunt & Huizinga (1999) model, has enabled us to identify the monetary aggregates that have a significant influence on the financing of the economy in the CEMAC countries.

According to our panel data analysis, reserves have a significant positive impact on credit to the economy, which in our model measures the financing of the economy. This result corroborates our initial hypothesis and the theory that deposits create credits. Moreover, the repatriation of net foreign assets is necessary for the financing of the economy, because their increase has a negative impact on the financing of the economy.

The paradox of our study is the result obtained on inflation, although not significant, because in economic theory it increases credit rationing, but we have a positive impact on financing.

In terms of our results, we recommend:

Increasing bank reserves, especially reserve requirements. The Central Bank can raise the rates applied to reserves, in order to better ensure refinancing;

With the surplus reserves, the Central Bank can create a guarantee fund for SMEs.

The Central Bank must continue to monitor the level of the banks' net foreign assets.

It is even desirable to determine a threshold to ensure better control of NEA.

The member states of the Union can create a community fund, financed by them, but managed as a private structure in order to encourage the intervention of banks at the level of productive enterprises.

BIBLIOGRAPHIC REFERENCES

Arouna Mopa (2008), *"La question du financement de l'économie camerounaise"*, www.cacistes.com/photos/file/article-aruna-mopa.pdf

Ary Tanimoune, N. and Plane, P. (2005), *"Performance et convergence des politiques économiques en zone franc"*, Revue française d'économie, Vol. XX, n° 1, pp. 235-268.

Avom, D. and Eyeffa Ekomo, S. M. L. (2007), *"Quinze ans de restructuration bancaire dans la CEMAC : qu'avons-nous appris ?"*, Revue d'économie financière, n° 189.

Avom, D. and Carmignagni, F. (2008), *"Economic growth and poverty reduction in*

Central Africa", Applied Economics, n° 4.

Africapractice, (2005), *"Access to finance: profiles of African SMEs"*, Jetro London.

Agénor P.R., Aizenman J., Hoffmaister A., (2004) *"The credit crunch in East Asia: What can bank excess liquid assets tell us"*. Journal of International Money and Finance 23, 27-49.

Agénor P.R., El Aynaoui K., (2009) *"Excess liquidity, bank pricing rules, and monetary policy"* Journal of Banking & Finance, Elsvier B. V.

Agénor P.R., El Aynaoui K., (2007). *"The transmission mechanism of monetary policy in Morocco: An analytical framework." Unpublished,* Bank Al Maghrib.

Aryeetey, E. (1998), *"Informal finance for private sector development in Africa"*, AfDB, *Economic Research Papers 41.*

Ashcraft A., McAndrews J., Skeie D., (2009) *"Precautionary reserves and the interbank market."* Staff Report No. 370, Federal Reserve Bank of New York.

Baltensperger, E. (1972), *"Costs of banking activities: interactions between risk and operating costs"*, *Journal of Money, Credit and Banking*, No. 4.

Banque de France (2006), *"L'essor des marchés de la dette publique en Afrique subsaharienne : le cas de l'UEMOA"*, in: *Rapport annuel sur la Zone Franc.*

BEAC - Bank of Central African States (2006), *Etudes et Statistiques*, n° 301, July-September.

World Bank (2006), *Doing Business 2007. How to reform.* Montreal, Quebec. 192 pages.

Bekolo-Ebe, B. and Ngango, G. (1989), *"Crise économique et impératif d'unité en*

Afrique", *Présence africaine*, n° 149/150, *Hommage à Cheik Anta Diop*, pp. 51 - 67

Bervas, A. (2006), *"La liquidité de marché et sa prise en compte dans la gestion des risques"*,

Revue de la stabilité financière, no 8.

Berg, E. (1993), *"L'intégration économique en Afrique de l'Ouest: problèmes et stratégies"*, *Revue d'économie du développement*, n° 2.

Bougthon, J. M. (1992), "Le franc CFA : une zone de fragile stabilité en Afrique*", Finance et développement,* December. pp. 34- 36.

Boyd, J. H. and Nicolo, G. D. (2005), "The Theory of Bank Risk Taking and Competition Revisited", *The Journal of Finance*, Vol. LX, No. 3, pp. 1329-1343.

CFPB - Centre International de Formation de la Profession Bancaire (2008), "Les Connaissances économiques", ITB 2nd year of studies. Paris: F. O. I. Système graphic.

Cheik Anta Diop (1960), *Les fondements économiques et culturels d'un Etat fédéral d'Afrique noire*. Paris: Présence africaine, 1974.

Chevallier - Farat, T. (1992), "Why do we need banks?", *Revue d'économie politique,* 102 (5), Sept-Oct, pp. 633-685.

Chouchane-Verdier, A. (2004), "Une analyse empirique de l'impact de la libéralisation financière en Afrique subsaharienne sur la période 1983-1996", *Revue Tiers Monde*, t. XLV, n° 179, juillet-septembre, pp. 6 17-641.

COBAC - Commission Bancaire de l'Afrique Centrale (1995), *Annual Report,* Fiscal Years 1993/1995, 2004, 2005, 2006.

Collange, C. and Plane, P. (1994), "Devaluation of the CFA Franc: the case of Côte d'Ivoire", *Economie internationale*, Vol. 58, 2, pp. 3-25.

United Nations Economic Commission for Africa, Central Africa Subregional Office (2007), *The Economies of Central Africa 2007 (The Links between Growth, Poverty and Inequality)*. Paris: Maisonneuve et Larose.

Dermine, J. (2005), "Restructuration internationale et diversification : le cas du risque- crédit", *Revue d'économie financière*, n°, pp. 267-280.

Diamond, D. and Dybvig, P. (1983), "Bank runs, deposit insurance, and liquidity," *Journal of Political Economy*, Vol. 91, No. 3.

Diatkine, S. (1996), *Institutions et mécanismes monétaires*. Paris: Armand Colin. 176 pages.

Ekomié, J.-J. (1999), "La convergence au sein de la Communauté Économique et Monétaire de l'Afrique Centrale (CEMAC)*", Revue Économie & Gestion*, vol. 1, n° 2, pp. 3-30.

Figuet, J.-M. (2000), "Le prêteur en dernier ressort international", *Revue d'économie financière*, n°

70, pp. 57-75.

IMF - International Monetary Fund (2007), "The DRC Financial Sector", *Country Report 0 7/329*.

Fouda Owoundi, J.-P. (2001), "Can the CFA Franc become a strong currency?*", Mondes en développement*, volume 29, n° 113/114, pp. 151-173.

Fouda Owoundi, J.-P. (2008), "La convergence des politiques économiques dans la zone francze quinze après: où en est-on?", *Working paper*, CEREG, University of Yaoundé II.

Freimer, M. and Gordon, M. (1969), "Why bankers ration credit", *Quarterly Journal of Economics*, No. 70.

Demirgüç-Kunt A. & Huizinga H. (1999) : "*Detreminants of commercial bank interest margins and profitability : some international evidence*" in World Bank Economic Review, vol.14, n° 2, pp. 379-408.

Doumbia S. (2009), "*Le sous-financement des enterprises dans un contexte de surliquidité bancaire : le paradoxe de l'UMEOA*" 11 es journées scientifiques du Réseau Entreprenariat, INRPME-AUF-AIREPME

Ewehart,C. and N. Valla (2008), "*Financial market liquidity and lender of last resort*", *Financial Stability Review*, special liquidity issue, no 11.

Giovanni A., (1994) "*Monetary policy, liquidity, and foreign exchange markets*", Journal of Monetary Economics, Elsvier B. V.

Guerrien B., (2002) " Dictionnaire d'analyse économique ", LA DECOUVERTE, p. 356-358.

Hsiao, C., (1986), "Analysis of Panel Data", Econometric society Monographs N0

11. Cambridge Universirty Press.

Khemraj T., (2007) "*Why do banks demand excess liquidity? Evidence from Guyana.*" MPRA Paper, University of Munich.

Lefilleur, J. (2007), " *Le financement des PME en Afrique Sub-saharienne : contraintes et perspectives de développement* ", *Horizons Bancaires,* n° 332, p. 67-74.

Mohanti M.S., Schnabel G., Garcia-Lima P., (2006) "*Banks and aggregate credit: What is new? In: The Banking System in Emergin Economies: How much Progress has been Made?*" BIS Papers No. 28, Bank for International Settlements.

Malo, D. and Koyadondri, L. (2006), "Analyse de l'offre et de la demande de produits et services de microfinance et stratégies pour la couverture des zones rurales défavorisées", in: PNUD/FENU/PAE/SFI

Mckinnon, R. I. (1973), *Money and Capital in Economic Development*. Washington, D. C: The Brookings institution.

Mckinnon, R. I. (1963), "Optimun currency Areas", *American Economic Review*, vol. 57, pp. 717-725.

Mundell, R. (1961), "A Theory of Optimun Currency Areas", *American Economic Review*, Vol. 51, pp. 657-665.

N'goma, J. M. B. (2000), "Analyse des chocs d'offre et de demande dans la zone CFA: une méthode structurelle d'autoregression vectorielle", paper presented at the 40th Annual Meeting of the Canadian Society for Economics, Montreal, May 17-18.

North, D. (1990), *Institutions, Institutional change and Economics Performance*, Cambridge University Press. 152 pages.

OECD, African Development Bank (2007), *African Economic Outlook*, OECD ed. 667 pp.

Ondo Ossa, A. (2004), "Les difficultés d'ajustement en zone franc africaine, le cas des pays de la BEAC", paper presented at the International Conference on "La réforme de la zone franc", Abidjan, October 28-29.

Poole, W. (1968), *"Commercial bank reserves management in a stochastic model", Journal of Finance*, No. 23.

Reinhart, C. and Tokatlidis, I. (2003), "Financial Liberalization: The African Experience", *Journal of African Economies*, vol. 12, pp. 53-88.

Ricol, R. (2008), "Report on the financial crisis", Mission entrusted by the President of the Republic in the context of the 2008 French Presidency of the European Union.

Saxegard, M. (2006), "Excess Liquidity and Effectiveness of Monetary Policy: Evidence from Sub-Saharan Africa", IMF *Working paper*, No. 06/115.

Schumpeter, J. A. (1912), *Theory of Economic Evolution*. Translated by J. J. Anstett. Paris: Dalloz, 1935. 371 pages.

Shaw, E. S. (1973), *Financial deepening in economic development*. New York: Oxford university Press.

Stasavage, D. (1996), "La Zone franc et l'équilibre budgétaire", *Revue d'économie du développement*, n° 4, pp. 145-178.

Stiglizt, J. and Weiss, A. (1981), "credit rationing in markets with imperfect information", *American Economic Review*, vol. 71

Wamba, H. and Tchamanbe-Djine, L. (2002), "Information financière et politique d'offre de crédit bancaire eux PME : cas du Cameroun", *Revue Internationale PME*, Vol 15, n° 4, pp. 87-113.

Williamson, O. (1985), *The Economic Institutions of Capitalism*. New York: Ed. Free Press.

Wanda, R. (2006), "Risques, comportements bancaires et déterminants de la surliquidité", Cahiers électroniques du CRECCI - IAE, Cahier 24-2007.

APPENDICES

Appendix 1: Fisher test

. xtunitroot fisher ce__y_, dfuller lags(0) Fisher-type unit-root test for ce__y_ Based on augmented Dickey-Fuller tests

Ho: All panels contain unit roots	Number of panels	=6
Ha: At least one panel is stationary	Number of periods	=21
AR parameter: Panel-specific	Asymptotics: T -> Infinity	
Panel means: Included		
Time trend: Not included		

Drift term: Not includedADF   regressions: 0 lags

Statistic p-value

		Statistic	p-value
Inverse chi-squared(12) P	3.2370		0.9936
Inverse normalZ2	.6932		0.9965
Inverse logit t(29) L*2	.8618		0.9961
Modified inv. chi-squared Pm	-1.7887		0.9632

P statistic requires number of panels to be finite.

Other statistics are suitable for finite or infinite number of panels.

<u>**Appendix 2**</u>: **Estimation of the Fixed Effects Model**

```
xtreg ce__y_ mpib__x1_ re__x2_ aen__x3_ infl__x4_ tx__x5_, fe
Fixed-effects (within) regression          Number of obs    =      99
Group variable: pays                       Number of groups =       6
R-sq:  within  = 0.6096                    Obs per group: min =     15
       between = 0.7612                                   avg =    16.5
       overall = 0.4910                                   max =      20
                                  F(5,88)        =    27.48
corr(u_i, Xb)  = 0.4335                     Prob > F        =   0.0000

------------------------------------------------------------------------------
    ce__y_ |    Coef.  Std. Err.     t   P>|t|    [95% Conf. Interval]

-------------+----------------------------------------------------------------
  mpib__x1_ |  380.5397  338.7794    1.12  0.264  -292.7132   1053.793
    re__x2_ |  1.003825  .1723336    5.82  0.000   .6613479   1.346301
   aen__x3_ | -.0226685   .040221   -0.56  0.574  -.1025992   .0572622
   infl__x4_| -.9532338  .7907612   -1.21  0.231  -2.524706    .618238
     tx__x5_|  .4353169  3.073969    0.14  0.888  -5.673551   6.544185
      _cons |  93.82249   76.5678    1.23  0.224  -58.33992   245.9849
-------------+----------------------------------------------------------------
    sigma_u |  214.96549
    sigma_e |  68.674497
        rho |  .90739201   (fraction of variance due to u_i)
------------------------------------------------------------------------------
F test that all u_i=0:    F(5, 88) =   106.83          Prob > F = 0.000
```

```
. xtreg ce__y_ mpib__x1_ re__x2_ aen__x3_ infl__x4_ tx__x5_, re
Random-effects GLS regression              Number of obs    =      99
Group variable: pays                       Number of groups  =       6
R-sq:  within  = 0.5087                     Obs per group: min =      15
       between = 0.7592                                  avg =     16.5
       overall = 0.5664                                  max =      20
Random effects u_i ~ Gaussian              Wald chi2(5)     =   121.47
corr(u_i, X)     = 0 (assumed)             Prob > chi2      =   0.0000

------------------------------------------------------------------------
    ce__y_ |    Coef.  Std. Err.    z   P>|z|   [95% Conf. Interval]
-------------+----------------------------------------------------------
  mpib__x1_ |  252.923   528.9436   0.48  0.633   -783.7875   1289.633
    re__x2_ |  2.673591  .3000141   8.91  0.000    2.085574   3.261608
   aen__x3_ | -.2947949  .0765424  -3.85  0.000   -.4448154  -.1447745
   infl__x4_ |  .7699456  1.958922   0.39  0.694    -3.06947   4.609362
    tx__x5_ |  7.254769  7.808124   0.93  0.353   -8.048873   22.55841
      _cons | -94.03951  177.8276  -0.53  0.597   -442.5752   254.4962
-------------+----------------------------------------------------------
    sigma_u |        0
    sigma_e |  68.674497
        rho |        0   (fraction of variance due to u_i)
------------------------------------------------------------------------
```

Appendix 4: tests of the variable effects model

. xttest0

Breusch and Pagan Lagrangian multiplier test for random effects

ce__y_[pays,t] = Xb + u[pays] + e[pays,t]

Estimated results:

```
        |    Var      sd = sqrt(Var)
--------+-----------------------------
  ce__y_|  69046.71      262.7674
      e |  4716.187       68.6745
      u |       0             0
```

Test: Var(u) = 0

chi2(1) = 395.73

Prob > chi2 =   0.0000

Country	years	CE (Y)	MPIB (X1)	RE (X2)	AEN (X3)	INFL (X4)	TX (X5)
1	1987	1077,04	0,18		-204,74	0,00	13,00
2	1987	29,38	0,17		16,73	-6,90	11,42
3	1987	184,00	0,20		-46,30	1,00	11,13
4	1987	293,30	0,21		-57,10	-1,00	11,13
5	1987	7,52	0,27		-3,94		14,13
6	1987	74,17	0,21		7,33		10,50
1	1988	1086,42	0,20		-117,95	0,00	13,46
2	1988	32,42	0,15	22,50	14,15	-4,00	12,25
3	1988	181,30	0,21		-42,90	-1,80	11,79
4	1988	255,40	0,22		-57,60	-8,60	11,79
5	1988	7,17	0,15		-5,51	-4,90	14,79
6	1988	72,95	0,16		12,20	-15,50	10,79
1	1989	1143,94	0,23		-192,84	0,00	15,00
2	1989	36,53	0,16	27,30	19,57	0,70	13,00
3	1989	188,50	0,19		-50,20	0,10	12,50
4	1989	215,50	0,34		-9,88	7,00	12,50
5	1989	8,26	0,11		-6,93	5,20	15,50
6	1989	61,42	0,17		22,17	-3,90	11,50
1	1990	816,31	0,20		-154,42	0,00	18,50
2	1990	35,62	0,16	34,20	18,25	-0,20	18,50

3	**1990**	154,93	0,21		-6,91	2,90	18,50
4	**1990**	219,47	0,17		20,78	7,60	18,50
5	**1990**	6,29	0,06		-6,11	2,70	18,50
6	**1990**	44,73	0,14		29,89	-3,30	18,50
1	**1991**	651,40	0,20		-139,90	3,20	18,15
2	**1991**	25,16	0,15	34,00	15,75	-2,20	18,15
3	**1991**	160,52	0,20		-16,20	-1,70	18,15
4	**1991**	230,04	0,18	5,62	37,93	6,90	18,15
5	**1991**	1,69	0,07		-4,63	-5,80	18,15
6	**1991**	52,39	0,15		20,35	7,50	18,15
1	**1992**	542,63	0,19		-172,33	-3,20	17,77
2	**1992**	21,11	0,15	31,52	16,16	-1,40	17,77
3	**1992**	76,30	0,17	4,09	-4,27	-3,90	17,77
4	**1992**	217,80	0,16	7,01	-23,25	-6,20	17,77
5	**1992**	2,31	0,08	0,84	-5,77	-6,80	17,77
6	**1992**	36,83	0,13		12,45	-3,20	17,77
1	**1993**	487,03	0,17	28,66	-225,80	-1,00	17,46
2	**1993**	20,47	0,18	27,69	24,04	-2,91	17,46
3	**1993**	82,40	0,16	3,84	0,40	4,90	17,46
4	**1993**	213,14	0,15	24,22	-26,87	0,50	17,46
5	**1993**	2,43	0,07	0,83	-7,39	3,87	17,46
6	**1993**	31,39	0,12	0,67	0,01	-6,90	17,46
1	**1994**	475,93	0,18	17,89	-295,88	32,00	17,50
2	**1994**	24,54	0,24	28,59	92,00	24,63	17,50
3	**1994**	91,05	0,16	3,09	13,11	42,39	17,50
4	**1994**	214,93	0,14	5,94	66,10	36,10	17,50
5	**1994**	2,97	0,12	1,47	-13,51	38,77	17,50
6	**1994**	35,33	0,10	0,61	14,03	43,72	17,50
1	**1995**	484,95	0,15	54,82	-328,70	9,10	16,00
2	**1995**	30,81	0,22	34,29	98,64	19,20	16,00
3	**1995**	100,28	0,15	9,68	23,04	9,40	16,00
4	**1995**	254,63	0,14	7,85	21,62	9,60	16,00
5	**1995**	4,09	0,14	1,25	-9,94	11,67	16,00
6	**1995**	39,38	0,13	1,98	48,79	9,27	16,00
1	**1996**	442,46	0,12	60,15	-280,80	3,90	22,00
2	**1996**	30,38	0,24	114,56	106,03	3,72	22,00
3	**1996**	113,11	0,14	12,05	33,43	7,50	22,00
4	**1996**	247,78	0,14	56,87	98,94	1,80	22,00

5	**1996**	7,15	0,12	0,62	-7,30	6,74	22,00
6	**1996**	52,94	0,14	6,17	55,08	11,32	22,00
1	**1997**	463,33	0,13	90,21	-181,97	4,80	22,00
2	**1997**	30,54	0,21	116,59	96,62	1,61	22,00
3	**1997**	131,75	0,15	7,41	23,39	16,60	22,00
4	**1997**	351,26	0,15	27,06	97,40	4,13	22,00
5	**1997**	13,00	0,06	1,95	-7,26	3,10	22,00
6	**1997**	58,53	0,13	10,08	57,05	5,56	22,00
1	**1998**	564,82	0,13	122,77	-172,61	3,20	22,00
2	**1998**	35,93	0,16	123,77	72,46	-1,89	22,00
3	**1998**	145,60	0,15	8,99	-29,75	-1,60	22,00
4	**1998**	364,52	0,17	48,12	-48,68	2,30	22,00
5	**1998**	14,88	0,08	1,49	1,59	7,80	22,00
6	**1998**	65,86	0,11	7,39	44,37	4,26	22,00
1	**1999**	590,20	0,13	61,78	-214,16	1,90	22,00
2	**1999**	43,40	0,17	108,85	75,63	-1,50	22,00
3	**1999**	173,39	0,15	14,48	4,98	3,60	22,00
4	**1999**	362,47	0,16	44,10	-46,59	-0,70	22,00
5	**1999**	21,32	0,08	4,38	10,12	0,60	22,00
6	**1999**	59,07	0,11	12,77	35,40	-8,00	22,00
1	**2000**	700,52	0,15	85,57	48,44	1,20	22,00
2	**2000**	38,91	0,17	83,71	79,51	3,10	22,00
3	**2000**	163,94	0,15	7,17	151,79	0,50	22,00
4	**2000**	401,61	0,15	27,47	173,74	0,50	22,00
5	**2000**	27,06	0,06	3,00	21,11	4,60	22,00
6	**2000**	65,28	0,13	10,13	33,60	3,80	22,00
1	**2001**	761,74	0,16	133,55	126,14	4,50	20,67
2	**2001**	42,47	0,16	91,13	63,65	3,80	20,67
3	**2001**	108,99	0,13	12,72	26,82	0,80	20,67
4	**2001**	471,80	0,16	34,78	-11,47	2,10	20,67
5	**2001**	36,59	0,05	5,11	61,85	8,80	20,67
6	**2001**	79,76	0,12	10,35	28,40	12,40	20,67
1	**2002**	834,45	0,18	210,98	298,33	2,83	18,00
2	**2002**	49,38	0,15	96,08	47,85	2,32	18,00
3	**2002**	66,41	0,14	105,99	29,71	3,00	18,00
4	**2002**	508,14	0,17	75,62	19,90	0,20	18,00
5	**2002**	54,22	0,07	10,37	103,85	7,60	18,00
6	**2002**	79,14	0,14	9,89	79,16	5,20	18,00
1	**2003**	907,77	0,17	315,01	257,66	0,60	18,00

2	**2003**	49,42	0,14	90,64	40,15	4,20	18,00
3	**2003**	81,74	0,14	30,07	-1,51	1,70	18,00
4	**2003**	466,66	0,17	56,10	64,67	2,30	18,00
5	**2003**	51,62	0,10	28,87	153,31	7,30	18,00
6	**2003**	98,09	0,12	12,89	46,06	-1,80	18,00
1	**2004**	904,89	0,17	202,37	354,99	0,30	18,00
2	**2004**	55,16	0,16	79,47	42,56	-2,05	18,00
3	**2004**	85,05	0,14	29,34	51,05	3,60	18,00
4	**2004**	422,91	0,17	54,19	275,53	0,40	18,00
5	**2004**	62,84	0,08	22,86	499,26	4,20	18,00
6	**2004**	92,85	0,11	28,59	55,82	-5,30	18,00
1	**2005**	976,84	0,17	301,04	497,56	1,90	17,67
2	**2005**	54,11	0,17	71,19	48,78	2,90	17,67
3	**2005**	86,14	0,14	37,44	458,34	2,50	17,67
4	**2005**	464,92	0,18	88,82	525,32	-0,20	17,67
5	**2005**	93,83	0,07	84,37	1240,65	5,00	17,67
6	**2005**	129,61	0,08	19,54	71,40	7,90	17,67
1	**2006**	999,46	0,17	404,02	1031,90	5,10	15,33
2	**2006**	56,43	0,15	77,52	36,00	6,60	15,33
3	**2006**	96,50	0,17	194,33	1035,29	4,70	15,33
4	**2006**	555,79	0,20	268,08	694,45	4,00	15,33
5	**2006**	129,45	0,07	179,77	1573,64	5,00	15,33
6	**2006**	136,53	0,11	83,03	258,68	8,10	15,33
1	**2007**	1083,06	0,19	605,68	1513,20	1,10	15,00
2	**2007**	59,07	0,14	70,05	24,99	0,96	15,00
3	**2007**	113,98	0,20	185,64	1102,80	2,50	15,00
4	**2007**	635,85	0,19	239,80	1098,93	4,80	15,00
5	**2007**	183,69	0,09	343,50	1800,20	5,50	15,00
6	**2007**	121,62	0,11	54,98	411,20	-7,40	15,00

1-Cameroon 2-RCA 3-Congo 4-Gabon 5-Equatorial Guinea 6-Chad

Printed by Books on Demand GmbH, Norderstedt / Germany